The Body Language of Children

The Body Language of Children

by
Suzanne Szasz

Foreword by
Dr. Benjamin Spock

W · W · NORTON & COMPANY · INC · NEW YORK

This book is lovingly dedicated to the memory of Dr. Dora
Hartmann, who encouraged me to know and trust myself.

I would like to thank several people who helped with
different aspects of this book:
Elizabeth Taleporos, Ph.D., a developmental psychologist,
for enthusiastically applying her knowledge and insight to
the marriage of text and photographs;
Sherry Huber, my editor, for her help;
James Mairs, for his continuing encouragement;
Anna W. M. Wolf, child care editor, to whom I am indebted
for our years of collaboration on picture stories dealing with
children's problems. Our work resulted in a book, *Helping
Your Child's Emotional Growth,* and in illustrating the Child
Study Association's *Child Care Encyclopedia.*
But, most of all, I want to thank all the families who
allowed me insight into their lives, to photograph their
intimate feelings and actions.

Library of Congress Cataloging in Publication Data

Szasz, Suzanne

    The body language of children

    1. Nonverbal communication (psychology).
    2. Infant psychology. 3. Parent and child.
    I. Title.
    BF723.N64S92 1978 155.4'13 78-7935

DESIGNER: ARNOLD SKOLNICK

ISBN 0 393 01171 2

1 2 3 4 5 6 7 8 9 0

CONTENTS

FOREWORD

By Benjamin Spock, M.D.

This book, made up of 192 vivid photographs and explanations, delights and moves me powerfully. If you love children—or even love just some of them—you'll have the same response.

When you and I take pictures of our children, we usually try to catch them laughing. Or we make funny faces and sounds to compel them to laugh. We want them to look at the camera and at us. We say they look cute this way.

I suppose the deeper meaning is that we yearn to have them happy always, no matter how unrealistic that hope is. We want to recall them later as responding joyfully to us. We want them to appear happy when we show their pictures to fond relatives and friends.

This desire for smilingness is part of our attitude toward our adult friends too. We ask them to say cheese when we take their pictures. And our candidates for office—from president to dog catcher—feel they must always be caught smiling in news photographs to win our confidence and votes.

To put it more sharply, we seem to want to forget and deny the negative feelings—anger, anxiety, jealousy, sorrow—so we try to keep them out of our pictures. Perhaps unconsciously and superstitiously we are trying to protect our children and friends from these painful emotions by this kind of magic.

But, when we ignore all the moods except happiness in our pictures, we leave out vital aspects of our children's personalities and experiences, aspects that we could learn from while our children are young, aspects that would fascinate us to recall when we look at their photographs in later years.

Suzanne Szasz does not focus exclusively or even predominantly on sweetly smiling babies, though she obviously likes them too. She takes pride in revealing the widest variety of personalities and moods in children, and she captures them in some of the dramatic moments of early life—a three-year-old's first encounter with the new baby, a fiery quarrel between two children, a parental tiff watched intently by their child, a saucy girl sticking her tongue out at the photographer.

Suzanne Szasz is not just a skillful photographer of children, she is a sensitive student of their feelings. She has worked with professionals in the field of child development and child guidance. But her shrewd observations of how children express their feelings through facial and bodily movements are her very own.

She has refined this knowledge through studying thousands of her own photographs.

She shows us examples of the universal meaning of elevated eyebrows and lowered eyebrows, of the raising of one shoulder in contrast to the raising of two, of the placing of a hand to the head, of the turning of the open palm upward in supplication or questioning.

She illustrates the skill with which children can imitate their parents' mannerisms, sometimes with subtle ridicule.

Suzanne Szasz is able to get her remarkably candid pictures by being around her subjects quietly, unobtrusively, and with the least possible equipment, until they accept her as part of the scene.

The value of this book is not simply that it makes us respond fondly to these children. Suzanne Szasz teaches us, through these pictures, to be aware, much more aware, of our children's feelings, and of what they are telling us through their facial and bodily expressions. To put it more emphatically, she helps us to overcome that blindness to children's feelings that most of us parents slip into.

We are sensitive to signs of physical illness in our children. We are quick to notice if they are getting close to danger—falls, fire, street accidents. We are always watching their behavior to see that they are being "good." But in the midst of these other preoccupations we tend to overlook their subtle feelings, to the detriment of our relationship with them.

Suzanne Szasz did not have to guess at the meanings of these children's expressions. She stayed with them long enough to get to know them and their life situations. Some of them she observed over a period of years.

I responded with particularly strong feelings to certain pictures: Elizabeth's security blanket had to be washed, but she has found it in the wash basin and is pressing it—soaking wet—to her face while she dreamily sucks her fingers. In the faces and bodies of two little girls watching television, there is distressing anxiety. There is a shift from fear to relieved hilarity in a group when the crisis in a Punch and Judy show has passed. A baby solemnly eats a flower. One-year-old Melissa's pouting and immobility mystifies her mother until it turns out she is upset by the feeling of the grass she's standing on for the first time. Chrissy sits on the toilet and shouts into the next room that she is ready for wiping. Edward at one and a half throws up his hands and purses his mouth to show that he wants no more vegetable. Sheila uses her arm to shut out the sight of her mother, who is telling her she must put her toys away, and then sticks her tongue out at her. Morgan jumps up and down in a rage to try to loosen his mother's grip on him. A young baby reaches out lovingly with finger and tongue to touch her brother's face. Allison, perched on a high stool and clinging to the rungs with her toes, shows delight in painting her easel picture. Chrissy lies with cheek pressed to the bedspread to get to the level of a wobbly kitten. Valerie covers her mother's eyes to keep her from admiring the new baby. A two-year-old steals a drink out of the baby's bottle. A girl scolded by her mother turns around in her misery and beats her doll. Scorn envelops a girl's face as she regards a picture being painted by another child.

A three-year-old in a huff trails her security blanket up the stairs to get away from a photographic session. A baby chortles with glee in her bathtub. A girl who has been told she can take off her dress unexpectedly takes off everything and runs ecstatically.

Whether you are fascinated with the meaning of children's deeper feelings or whether you just enjoy looking at pictures of expressive babies and young children, you'll love this book. You'll keep going back to look at it again—as I do.

I
Introduction to Body Language

Feelings and "gut-level" emotions are often best expressed in ways that do not use words. The true nature of our inner feelings may be hidden by words. We observe this every day of our lives as we listen to someone tell us something while their body language conveys something quite different.

While most people have not really thought through some of the issues raised in this book and its photographs, we actually understand body language more than we realize. Often we can guess at a person's mood without spoken words. A down-turned mouth, slightly drooping shoulders, and a furrowed brow communicate unhappiness quite clearly even if we did not stop to analyze exactly *how* we came to understand what we saw.

This book, essentially, is about children and parents—about their feelings, their interaction, and communication through body language.

I hope that you will be able to see and feel the emotions portrayed in my photographs, and that this may help enhance your own perceptions about people and about how children develop. It is exciting to see how children and parents communicate their needs, fears, hopes, and joys to each other.

The body language of children is the most reliable way of understanding their feelings and desires. Especially with preverbal children, body language is important. For example, parents have to learn to distinguish between a hunger cry, a lonely cry, or a bored cry by observing the infant's physical clues.

A good parent-child relationship demands that parents quickly tune in to their children's nonverbal language and, at the same time, that children learn what their parents's body language is telling them.

Before we look at how different feelings are usually expressed in body language, see whether you can tell what is going on in the next few photographs.

Pinpointing Body Language

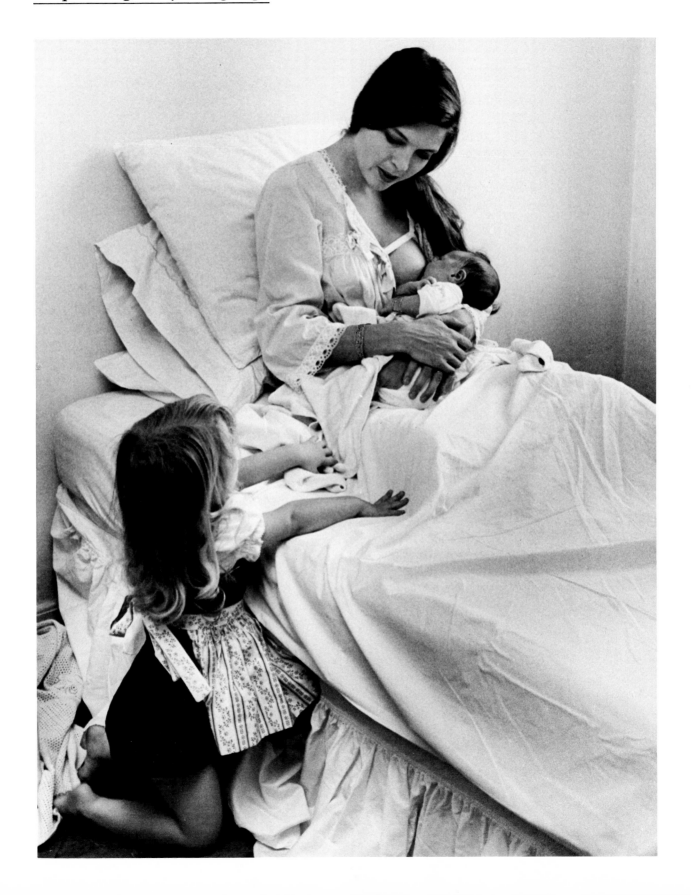

Looking at this photograph, you probably already formed some ideas about the people in it. But exactly *how* did you arrive at your opinion? Probably by synthesizing the manifestations of body language evident in the scene.

What exactly are the signs of body language that tell you that this is a mother who loves her children, who is able to give of herself to both? What do you see that shows you that Maya, the three-year-old watching her mother nurse the new baby, has many conflicting feelings?

Mother's arms and hands are completely relaxed, encircling the baby.

Her head is leaning toward both children: forward toward the baby; sideways toward Maya. Her facial expression is calm, serene, attentive toward Maya. Note her clear brow, slightly upturned mouth.

Maya is kneeling near the bed, just as close as she can get to it. Her left hand is caressing the blanket; but her right hand is pushing tensely against her mother. Her ambivalence is expressed by these different hand positions. "I love you, Mummy," says the one hand; "I am angry at you and the baby," says the other.

IS THIS CHILD READY TO GO TO SLEEP?

The foot over the bed's railing suggests that he wants to get out of bed. But the head and the rest of the body do *not* strain toward the outside; two-year-old Johnny seems to have accepted that it is bedtime and is slowly turning for comfort to his teddy bear.

So, in spite of the overall first impression, the answer to our question is yes; Johnny is ready to go to sleep soon.

WHAT IS THIS CHILD'S MOOD?

Has she turned her back in anger, or is she happily occupied? The answer:
Amy, age three, is playing with a new toy, and her parents glancing in at her
and seeing only this symmetrical, well coordinated back view, can go back
to their own pursuits: Amy is relaxed and content with what she is doing.

WHAT ARE THESE CHILDREN REALLY LIKE?

I especially appreciate the permission of the parents of these two children to show you their photographs.

Would you have been able to guess that the little clown's radiant smile covers problems serious enough to warrant treatment—but that tragic-looking Sandy's dark mood was only momentary?

That is why it is so important to know the circumstances in which photographs were taken. Only in the context of the whole situation is a look or gesture meaningful. Therefore throughout the book I will describe the exact background of the pictures shown.

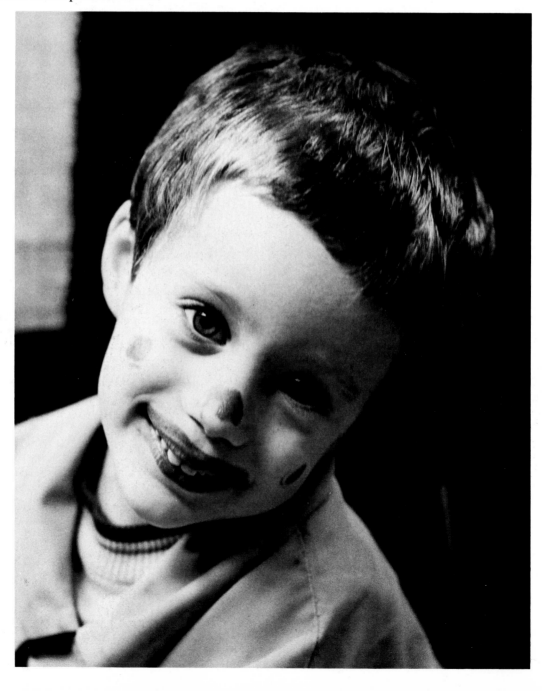

ABOUT CHILDREN'S REACTION TO THE CAMERA

I try to take photographs as if I were invisible. But I am aware
that my presence must affect the situations I photograph somewhat.

I don't talk to the children much; I don't try to "make friends"
with them. I let them react in their usual way to the people around
them. I never use flash or more photo equipment than absolutely
necessary. Because I work this way, I have come to feel that
whatever effect photography has on the situation, it only serves to
intensify, not change the children's feelings. My goal is the same as
the one that child psychologist Jean Piaget once described as his
aim: *to capture what is hidden behind the immediate appearance
of things.*

I rarely take photographs of people I haven't met; but, wandering
around at a folk music festival, I couldn't resist Maya's beauty and
focused my camera on her. As I did so, she clutched her mother's
knees and gave me a long, searching look. It seems to express the
slightly fearful interest that we all feel when a camera "takes" a
picture (and, according to many myths, a piece of our soul with it).
I am always conscious of the hostile language of photography: we
speak of "taking" or "shooting" a picture.

Children and the Camera

Being photographed makes most of us question ourselves; but we overcome this moment of doubt, put on our best smile, and try to radiate self-confidence and friendliness. Most children have not yet learned these tricks and they let us see their true feelings much more often than grownups do.

I feel that Minty, age four, is saying with her eyes that she is not sure this person with the camera will like her. At the same time, she seems to be opening her soul to us through the way she keeps her eyes wide open.

When one sees such "open" eyes, it is hard to remember that—except for the slightest dilation of the pupils—eyes themselves cannot change expression. Only the surrounding muscles make the eyes the mirror of the soul.

I came upon three-year-old Adam dressed in his father's old shirt. What does his body language say? One hand is lifted to his mouth, indicating hesitation and shyness; his other hand is holding the beloved shirt protectively, his whole pose and facial expression neutral but friendly. He is both intrigued and flattered by the photographer's attention.

I followed the development of these identical twins for several years. Their parents' account of them and a psychological test given to them at a later date both agreed with what this picture shows: Marina—on the left—was always the optimist, Tatiana the pessimist.

As they grew older, they came to look more and more different, illustrating how lines form differently in faces that are expressing predominantly joyful thoughts or predominantly sad or anxious thoughts.

UNIVERSAL GESTURES

The basic emotions of humans—happiness, sadness, disgust, fear, and hostility—are expressed in nearly identical ways of body language all over the world. Certain parts of our bodies, such as the eyebrows, shoulders, and hands, seem to convey specific messages that are clear to everyone.

Eyebrow Language

One eyebrow lifted expresses disbelief; two eyebrows lifted, surprise; eyebrows lowered, suspicion and mistrust.

In the photograph on the opposite page, both of Minty's eyebrows shoot up as she hears something she cannot believe and that surprises her. The resulting furrowing in her forehead also adds a note of displeasure to her face.

Shoulder Language

One shoulder raised means "I don't care" or "I don't know"; two shoulders raised denote fear; squared shoulders show determination; and lowered, rounded shoulders seem to be sagging under a real or imagined burden.

Six-year-old Alexandra always shrugs her left shoulder when baffled by a difficult question.

The English language has many expressions that take into account the most commonly observed body language. "Giving someone a cold shoulder" is one of them.

In the photograph on the opposite page, Chrissy, age four, is illustrating this saying. After she and her brother quarreled about which soft drink each would have, she turned around and raised her right shoulder as if to say "See if I care!"

Hand Language

Hands express many emotions. They point accusingly; they are raised menacingly; the palms can turn upward in a begging or questioning movement; they can wave exuberantly; they clench into a fist with tension; arms can be folded in self-protection.

We will be observing many of these hand movements through this book; here are just two easy-to-recognize hand signs.

Betsy, age five, is overwhelmed by the task ahead of her; she is raising her hand to her head in a movement signifying "Oh boy!"

Six-year-old Kathleen has just discovered that something is wrong with her complicated mathematical computation. Her hand flies to her head and starts to scratch it, expressing her efforts at solving her problem. Her brow is furrowed, her mouth turned down; it is obvious that she has not yet come up with the right answer.

Hand Language

Studying the behavior of mentally disturbed children can help us to a better understanding of normal children, because their gestures are so exaggerated as to be quite clear. In these photographs we see the hands of children who view the whole world as a dangerous place where they have to defend themselves against assaults. They use their hands to shut out what they don't want to hear and see, and to protect what they consider their most vulnerable parts.

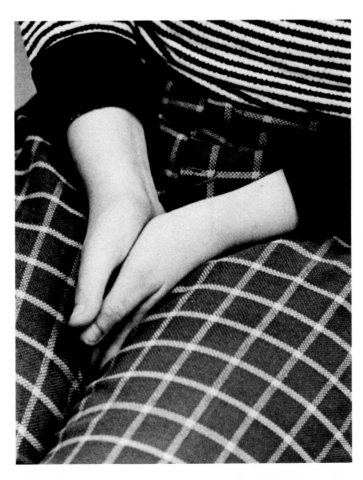

II
Feelings

1. WARMTH

Warmth is expressed in body language by getting close; by touching; by leaning, and by getting on the same level with the other person.

No wonder the word "warmth" also means the ability to love and communicate. After all, the first love a newborn knows *is* the warmth of the mother's body. Feeding provides an ideal time for a mother to transmit this all-important warmth to her baby.

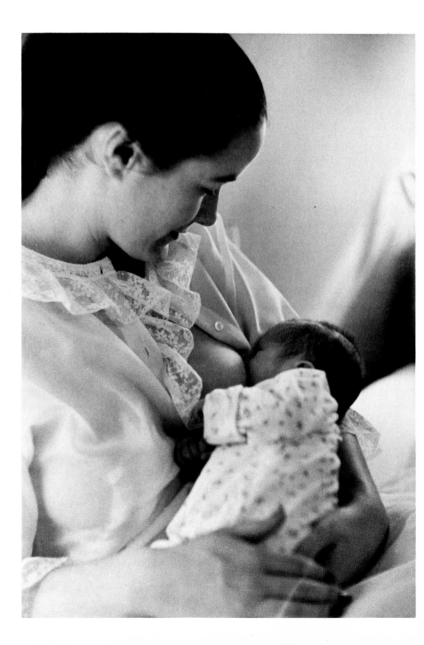

Rooming-in allowed Melissa to enjoy her mother's
warm embrace right from the start of her life, in the
hospital. Satisfaction is written all over her face; her
body is snuggled against her mother's body; she is
relaxed and seems to be dreaming happily.

Body Play

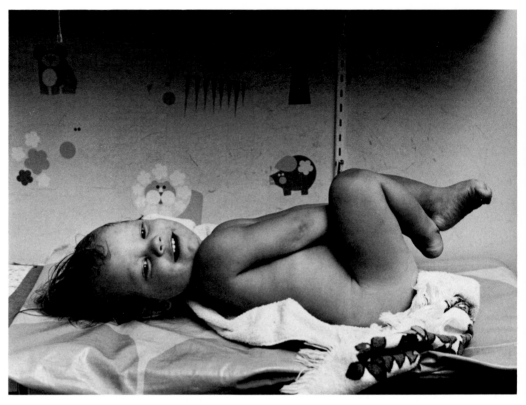

Most children, having enjoyed physical affection from their parents or nurse, will want to explore their bodies and feel upset when restricted from doing so by disapproval and reproaches.

Twelve-month-old Andrew is playing with his body after a bath; his smile shows that his mother and father have not frowned upon his doing so. His toes are curled in pleasure.

This kind of parental attitude will encourage a relaxed approach to sexuality and will spare misconceptions and unnecessary guilt later.

Father is home doing some office work, while Debi, age one, is playing at the other end of the sofa. She stays there happily for a long time, because every now and then her father turns away from his work and gives her signs of his attention by leaning toward her and talking to her. She responds with a happy smile; she has not understood the words, only the preverbal, universal language of his body leaning toward her.

Three-year-old Gerrett is unhappy that the car ride is over; his friend Wendy is trying to comfort him with her gentle supporting touch and by leaning toward him instinctively.

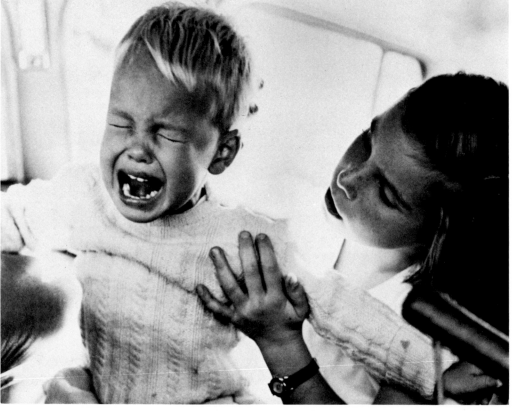

Longing for Warmth

Pets, whether real or stuffed, are a wonderful source of warmth and tenderness.

Janie, age four, is expressing her warm feelings by encircling her soft, cuddly teddy bear with love. She touches her cheek to his and presents a picture of roundness—as opposed to the angularity with which separateness and rejection are expressed.

Whenever four-year-old Amelia gets a bit tired or lonely, she curls up with her cat, nose to nose, their bodies touching; Amelia is smiling, the cat purring gently.

Soft objects—usually blankets—serve a good purpose. When Mother is not there, children can turn to them for comfort and at the same time enjoy the sensual pleasure of touching.

While I was doing a picture story on three-year-old Elizabeth and her security blanket, her mother washed it and so the child had to do without it for a short while. A few minutes later, I found Elizabeth in the bathroom, where the blanket was soaking, pressing the wet object to her face. Every muscle was involved in her effort to be close to her beloved blanket.

Warm Friendships

In most children's lives there comes a time when another child—usually of the same age and sex—becomes a very important person; they whisper, hug, and cling together endlessly. Amelia and Alison, both four years old, are neighbors and play together a lot, often expressing their warmth by touching. While rolling around the rug, they find themselves in an unusual position, seeing their faces upside down; this adds to their merriment.

Boys are usually less willing to express their warm feelings; but there are exceptions.

Perhaps the fact that both Benjamin and Mark—six years old—are each twins makes them used to physical closeness; they are inseparable in school. Here they are sitting in music class in a harmonious, parallel way.

Observing the photograph closely, we find one incongruous movement. How can we explain Benjamin's pointing, so-called "accusing finger"? It would signify anger or at least tenseness. In this case, it was probably evoked by the song he was singing. So we can ignore the pointing finger and accept the predominance of warmth and harmony expressed in all other ways by the two boys.

2. FEARS AND ANXIETY

The body language in which fear is expressed is unmistakable; fully opened eyelids, furrowed brows, a violently downturned mouth, and general muscular tenseness.

Fear of Strangers and of the Dark

This is one of a series of photographs I took of John, who was going through a stage identified by psychiatrist Dr. René Spitz as "Eight-months-anxiety." Actually, he says, it is a sign of intelligence and positive development that the baby is starting to recognize strangers as separate and different from his mother and the people who usually care for him. The unknown evokes the fear of strangers in him. The depth of these fears can be gauged by the strong body language.

The fear of darkness and the resulting reluctance to go to sleep is clearly visible on another John's face and body. At around age two, he has started to bite his lip, stare wide-eyed, and hold on to the bedrail with his hands whenever bedtime arrives.

To get this picture of him and to document his daily battle with bedtime, I spent two evenings and nights in his home. It was hard for me not to offer consolation when I, instead of the mother he asked for, came into his room; but this is the closest I could come to showing how a child feels alone, afraid of the dark.

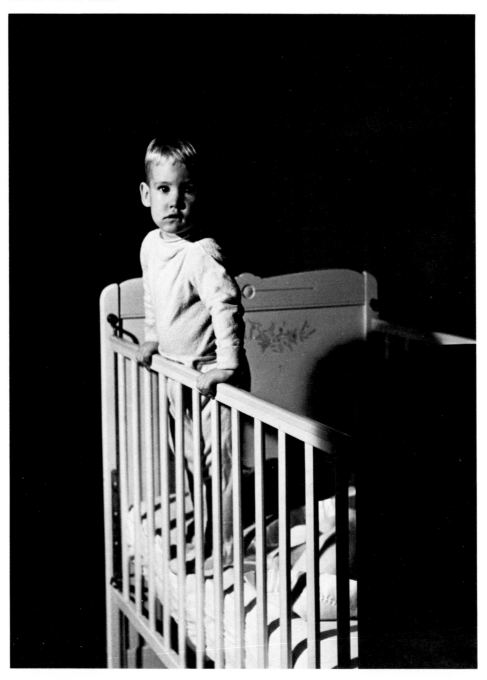

Anxiety

Have you ever wondered why all babies love to play peek-a-boo and laugh
with such abandon when their mother's face reappears? It seems that young
babies think that when someone is hidden from their view, that person is
gone, maybe forever. The anxiety shows in their whole tense demeanor.

Look at one-year-old Sheila's begging, palm-up right hand, her downturned
mouth, her left hand holding on to the bed for support.

And see her just a few seconds later, when her mother's face reappears:
her right hand palm down now, her left waving jubilantly, her mouth
turned upward in a big smile.

Sheila's reaction is perhaps a bit unusual for her age; most babies have
been playing this game for six months or more, so by the time they reach
twelve months, they are more relaxed and sure that mother will reappear.
Sometimes they even initiate the game.

Facing Strangers

Two-year-old Billy is being held tenderly by his mother, to give him a chance to get used to the idea that she has to leave him for a few hours with a babysitter.

His lower lip is pushed down and out, but he is "keeping a stiff upper lip" to keep from crying. He is not an especially sensitive or fearful child; just an expressive one, on whose face we can read how most children feel about being left for a while by their mothers.

Even at age four, Charlie is glad to hang on to his mother for a few moments, while he looks over the people at the party they have come to. Thus reassured, he will soon venture forth and have a good time. But every fifteen minutes or so, he will reappear to make sure that his parents are still there.

Three-year-old Chrissy's feelings of anxiety at the sight of strangers are well under control but still visible. Her eyebrows are drawn up and her eyelids pulled into a round shape.

She has found a little nook between a cupboard and a highchair, where she can "hide" until she feels ready to join the guests.

Shyness, Guilt and Fears

Betsy has taken refuge in a wingchair. It is her first day of school and she is worried about the new experience. Her hand is near her mouth for support and comfort, something that six-year-olds usually do only in moments of stress. Her eyes are wide open and reflect not only shyness but a certain amount of hostility too. This is a usual but rarely acknowledged component of shyness.

"If I withdraw, I'm protected; I won't be found out and I can't get into trouble."

Of all my photographs of fears, this is the one that best shows the connection between guilt and fear.

Adam, age six, left alone with his baby brother, played a little rough with him. (I was standing nearby, but, absorbed in his thoughts and feelings, he never noticed me.)

When his mother returns, he pulls back with fear

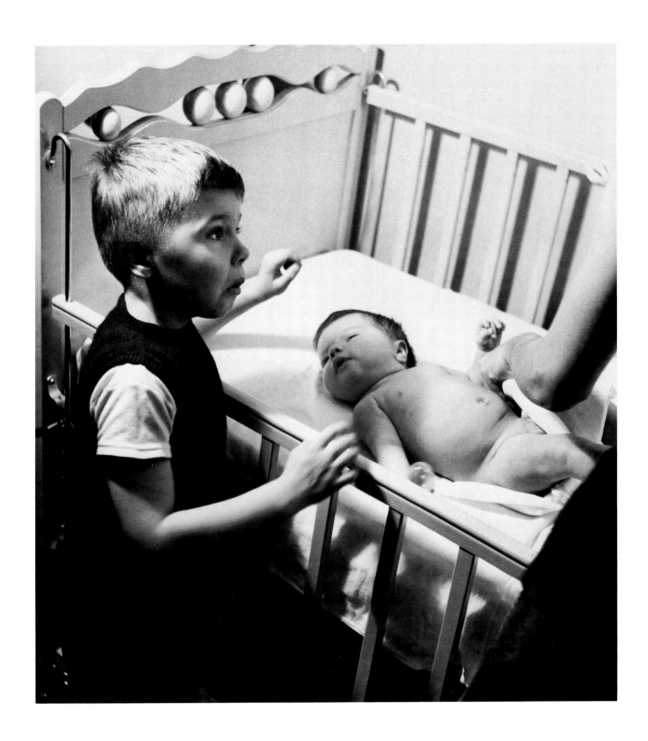

and guilt written all over him. It is not what he actually *did* that causes these feelings, but what he *wished to do*.

It is interesting that his arms fly into a position that we associate with "I give up!" and his mouth seems to form the "ooh" of pain and surprise.

Seeing nothing wrong, except Adam's strong reaction to her entrance, his mother is puzzled as to what happened.

All pet owners are familiar with the same scene: we come home to a cat or dog that exhibits a guilty conscience by hugging the ground, pulling back ears, making its fur stand on end, literally broadcasting that it has done something wrong while we were gone.

Fear of Doctors, Haircuts

Terry, age four, has been to the dentist before, and both she and her mother keep assuring each other that there is nothing to be afraid of. This takes a lot of doing on Mother's part, as she herself is afraid of dental work; but she tries not to communicate this fear to her daughter.

When the door opens and it is Terry's turn, she looks at her mother and asks: "You're coming too, Mummy?" She can barely contain her tears. Her mouth is forming the familiar "ooh," her eyebrows are raised, her forehead furrowed. Yet, holding on to Mother's hand, she submits to having a small cavity drilled and filled.

Terry's fear of the dentist is nothing compared to Leslie's, age five (opposite). Even though she has only come to have a haircut, this child is *terrified*. She is biting her lip and screaming alternately; pulling back toward her mother's body.

It seems like an irrational fear, for, after all, a haircut doesn't hurt. Children often have these fears, connected with increasing awareness of their bodies and the fear of losing parts of themselves.

Still, the strength of Leslie's reaction shows that the reality has little to do with her terror. Her fear seems too high a price to pay for a professional haircut and maybe her mother should try to cut Leslie's hair herself, at home, until her daughter's fears have lessened.

Children's Fears and TV

Most children love and easily understand fairy tales in which the wicked are punished in a cruel and explicit way, but they are scared of TV programs that shoot and hurt people. Television alternately reports reality and shows make-believe; the children see that adults often believe what they see on television, so why shouldn't the children feel convinced that what they are looking at is compellingly, frighteningly real too?

The distinction between reality and fantasy is only begun to be perceived with mental development around the ages of two and a half to three years.

In a recent survey, Dr. Nicholas Zill (Temple University's Institute for Survey Research) found that the more hours children spend watching TV, the more fearful they are.

My photographs seem to bear this out. The body language is clear: downturned mouths, staring eyes, tensed muscles. This is entertainment??

Catharsis at the Puppet Show

These children, sitting in the dark at a puppet show performance, are upset over the fate of Judy when she is threatened by Punch. Their older brother Howard has seen it all before, so he comforts his little sister, whose mouth is distorted with fear and who is clinging to him for consolation. His other sister too has her eyes wide open, her mouth and body tense.

But a few minutes later, the play has been resolved in the classical way of age-old stories: the innocent escape, the guilty are punished. The explosiveness of the children's relief shows the depth of their former worry: now their mouths are wide open in laughter, all their muscles relaxed.

3. CURIOSITY

During the years from approximately three to six, children's curiosity is at its height. There are several possible reasons why this is so. The Freudian concept says that children at this age are preoccupied with resolving their love-hate relationship with their parents. They become curious about anything that will help sort out these mysteries and conflicts.

Another point of view, such as that expressed by Dr. Margaret Mahler, is that by the age of three, children have basically resolved their separation anxiety. They are now free to explore their environment with a basic sense of trust and confidence.

In any case, discouraging the need to know can turn eager children into uninterested, bored adolescents. Early curiosity should be channeled toward exploration and study.

Curiosity is the drive behind children's desire and need to learn about the new things that confront them every day. Puzzlement results when the tasks seem too big, the challenges out of reach.

Curiosity and puzzlement are expressed in body language by staring and leaning; also by touching and tasting.

Three-year-old Gerry expresses his curiosity and puzzlement over his five-day-old baby sister with wide-open eyes and a slightly pursed mouth. He also emphasizes his interest by the position of his whole body and by leaning as close as possible to the baby's face.

The longer one looks at this photograph of nine-month-old Michele, the more one would like to know what puzzled or fascinated her so much. Her extremely wide-open eyelids and the constricted mouth give an impression of concentration, of wanting to find out about everything, of being eternally surprised by all the new occurrences in her life.

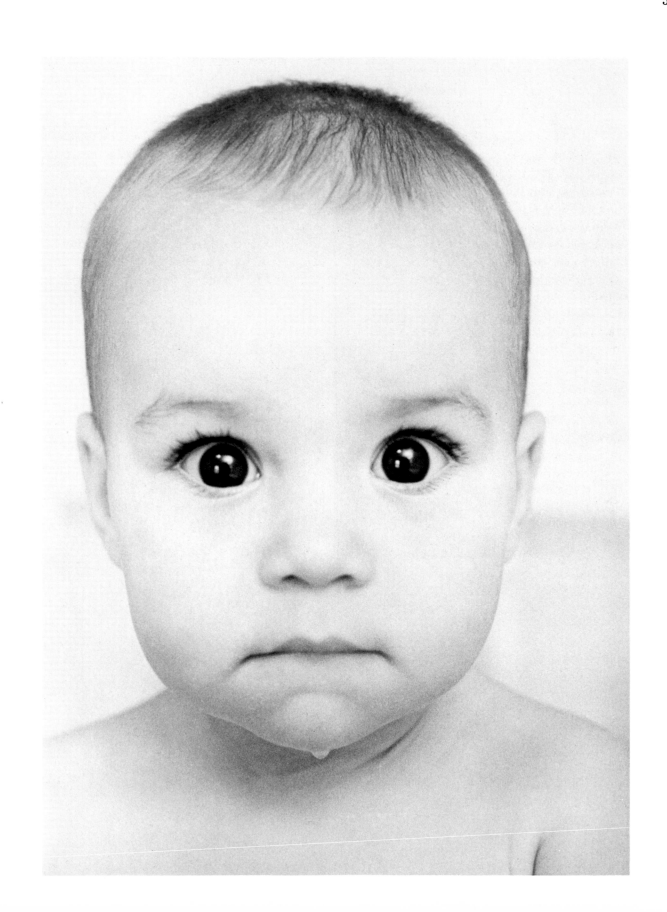

How Do Things Work?

It is amusing to see a child express his feelings with gestures that have become clichés, such as scratching the head to express puzzlement.

Adam cannot figure out how to put on his pajamas—so he scratches his head for a while, then gives up and calls his mother to help him.

Other children, less relaxed and more impatient, easily become frustrated in similar situations. Possibly they are being pushed to do well too fast and they panic when a puzzling problem proves too difficult for them.

Still others never want to try new things, perhaps because they have not found anyone willing to teach them simple tasks well and patiently.

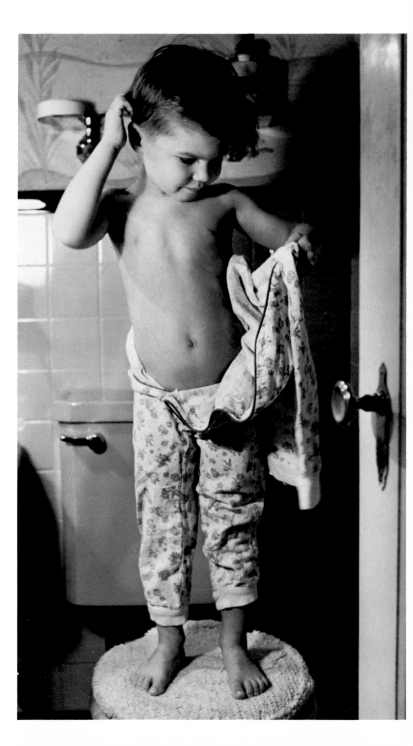

What better toy for a four-year-old than an old alarm clock that doesn't work anymore? Now Adam can take it apart, see how the hands work, and satisfy his curiosity.

Oral Curiosity

In their first year, most children exhibit oral curiosity, some more consistently than others. As it is very difficult to make children's surroundings completely safe—especially when they venture outdoors—this can be very dangerous. Understanding body language can save many a situation.

I know parents who start yelling "No! NO!" even before their child's hand has had time to reach his mouth in order to explore some fascinating substance. One mother told me that she had learned to recognize the special way in which her daughter crawled toward the houseplants when she was going to try to suck on the leaves (a veritable passion for a few weeks).

Morgan always wanted to put everything in his mouth, except what most children put there: his fingers. He never sucked his thumb, but everything else had to be tasted. At seven months, I caught him exploring the hose to his bathtub by putting it in his mouth. A few months later, when he first explored the garden, he wanted to taste all the flowers.

One-year-old David asked for a taste of his older sister's lunch. Now that he has tried it, he is puzzled by the flavor, one he never experienced before. The pursing of his lips indicates that he is disappointed.

The Dangers of Curiosity

In their first year, children learn more than they ever will again in any one year of their lives. Their curiosity drives them to see, touch, and taste everything. It is hard to draw the line between stunting children's healthy curiosity and letting them be exposed to real dangers. It is not excessive to worry about household accidents; there are far too many of them.

Learning to read children's minds by understanding their body language can be immensely helpful.

One-year-old Johnny has made his way to an electrical outlet, but his mother is alert. Just as he gets ready to pull at the cord, her sharp "NO!" stops him. His hands fly away from the coveted object; he draws back and looks up at her guiltily. Many, many similar warnings will be necessary until Johnny learns what is safe to explore. Meanwhile, his mother is relying on her ability to recognize an "extra special" look he gets on his face when he is contemplating another escapade.

Later on, children will often verbalize the familiar "NO" as they are doing the forbidden activity. Selma Fraiberg talks about this when she discusses the process by which children internalize a sense of conscience.

The one most common form of body language expressing puzzlement is the hand raised to the mouth. The next five photographs all show children doing this.

Sarah is only a year old. I never observed her parents using this gesture, so she cannot have learned it from them. It must be part of her inborn biological heritage. Charles Darwin observed that six basic emotions—happiness, sadness, surprise, anger, fear, and disgust—elicit the same expression in humans, from early infancy on, and in nearly all cultures.

Maya, age three, is trying to figure out whether she really wants a sip of her mother's coffee. Her mother says she won't like it, because it is bitter and strong. In a few moments, Maya will decide that she'd rather see for herself—with disappointing results.

Finger Language

All three of these children are in school, trying to solve problems; it seems to help them think to put their fingers in their mouths.

The first two are pondering the answer to a question the teacher posed.

The child opposite is confronted by a relatively new problem. She is attending a so-called "free school," where she is supposed to figure out what she wants to do with her time; what she would like to study that day. Her teacher is trying to give five-year-old Tami all the help he can. He is evidently getting impatient, but Tami is still puzzled.

4. NEGATIVE FEELINGS

The emotion can be called defiance, reluctance, negativism, or frustration. Some people speak of it as the "NO" period or the "Terrible Twos." Whatever the exact definition, the body language is explicit. From the hunched shoulders of a little girl unwilling to walk on grass to the full-fledged temper tantrum of a three-year-old who refuses to go to bed, they all give vent to their feelings in recognizable ways.

In this stage children wrinkle their brows, purse their lips, hunch their shoulders, and flail with their arms and legs. Some use their hands to hide what they don't want to see or cover their ears to shut out what their parents say.

Sometimes it takes real detective work to find out what bothers a one-year-old child whose vocabulary doesn't reach far and who just keeps standing there, immovable and obviously upset. In this case, it turned out that Melissa, who had never walked on grass before, found the sensation unsettling and wanted to be taken to a smoother surface to walk on.

The achievement of toilet training usually coincides with the worst of the "NO" stage— and no wonder. The discipline that toilet training requires doesn't come easily. Even with all that we know about the perils of rushing this stage, toilet training still causes many a battle and strong emotions on both sides.

Two-and-a-half-year-old Chrissy is announcing that she is ready; her expression leaves no doubt that she was not too happy about performing her "duty."

Refusal

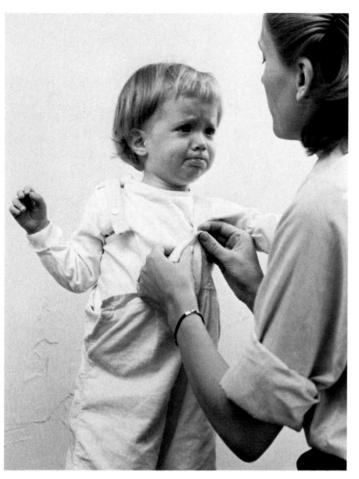

Two-year-old Amy doesn't like to get dressed; she protests in words and by knitting her forehead, pushing out her lower lip, and making her mother know that she feels put upon. But her right hand seems to be raised less in protest than in a patient, helpful gesture for completing the dressing process.

Amy is well on the way to learning one of the unpleasant facts of life: one has to get dressed in the morning.

No detective work is necessary to understand that neither Robin nor Edward wants to eat what is put before him.

Five-year-old Robin just sits there quietly, his vegetables uneaten; but his mouth is pulled into a tight small circle as if to say: "Nothing will pass through this tiny opening." His eyes are watching to see if his mother will notice. Mother knows it won't hurt her healthy son to skip some of his food once in a while, so she ignores his tactic.

This reasonable parental attitude seems to have eliminated a lot of hysterical eating scenes common when I was a child and a plate had to be clean without fail. Now many parents worry if their children eat too much.

Edward, aged one and a half, pulls away from his meal, throws up his hands, purses his mouth; evidently the experiment with a new vegetable is not a success.

Accepting the Inevitable

It is two years later and Edward, now three and a half, is sitting in the barbershop. He is not pleased; but he *is* resigned to having a haircut. It would be hard to describe in words exactly what he is doing with his mouth to express both these emotions, but we can understand.

The haircut was accomplished without too much fussing on his part.

I have spent many days with young mothers whose lives seem to be one round after another of argument and battle with their children. By late afternoon, I often notice that out of sheer exhaustion, they want to ignore the rules they set down in the morning. They know that it will lead to more trouble to be inconsistent—but they will give anything for a little peace. They tell me that if they engage in one more battle of wills that day, they know they will go overboard and scream instead of arguing gently.

It is close to suppertime; Louise has told her daughter Sheila that she will have to stop playing in five minutes. But Sheila, three, wants to go on playing.

When her mother approaches, she raises her arm to her eyes to hide her mother's unwelcome presence. Louise manages to stay friendly and suggests that they put the toys away together. No cooperation from Sheila! She moves away and sticks out her tongue in a well-known gesture of defiance. Sheila will have to be bodily carried to have her hands washed, and then to the dinner table. This is done in a firm but friendly way, not an easy attitude to maintain all day, every day.

Still, children need clear limits and a sense of order in their environment and help in learning self-control. This is called discipline, which all children need to develop into happy, constructive adults.

Temper Tantrums

It is especially painful to handle a recalcitrant child in public. Many mothers are afraid to "create a scene" and so they let their children get away with behavior in public that they would not tolerate at home.

When nothing else seems to work, and it is time to go home, a child will have to be shown who is stronger. He may kick and scream, but part of him will welcome the feeling that a strong but benevolent grownup watches over him.

Right now, two-year-old Morgan is yelling, jumping up and down, trying to loosen his mother's grip. Mother's knitted brow shows that she is upset; but she knows that she is asking Morgan to do something that is reasonable and unavoidable; and losing her own temper would just aggravate the situation.

Cindy has been a trying child for the past few months. Her mother can't wait for her to grow out of this "terrible two" stage. Her own expression and tense grip indicate that her patience is wearing a bit thin. Like most children in the clutches of a temper tantrum, Cindy seems twice as strong as she usually is, flailing her arms, stamping her feet and yelling all at the same time. It is very tempting to give in to such strong outbursts: but experts warn that if that happens, a child will learn that temper tantrums *work* to manipulate their parents, and there will be more tantrums than before.

Temper Tantrums

Defiance

Chrissy, five, is evidently past the stage where one can argue with her; she has probably forgotten what made her unhappy a while ago, yet still cannot stop her tantrum.

Luckily, it is a rare occurrence. Her mother comforts her in such cases, tells her she loves her, and slowly the original demand fades from Chrissy's memory.

She did not get what she wanted, but neither was she punished for expressing her wishes, even in an unacceptable way.

It is hard to find the thin line between forbidding children to express their feelings and allowing temper tantrums to be the rule when something goes against their wishes. Many parents and teachers, getting the message from the children's body language that something is brewing inside them, wisely encourage strenuous play-acting or dancing and singing, to drain and relieve these emotions without having to repress them.

Seven-year-old Isabel and her friends are doing just that, with great glee and abandon. During the wild music and general foolishness, Isabel can express her mixed feelings about my presence without having to be impolite to me or pretend that she likes me.

Or perhaps I am just a handy target against whom to express some previous frustration.

5. LOVE AND SEXUALITY

The existence of love is inseparable from its tangible manifestation: body language. Hands touch, bodies lean, faces smile, eyes sparkle.

When I was going through my photographs to see at what age a baby can express love, I found that as early as two months, Billy responded to his mother's love.

Psychologists generally agree that true social, interactive smiling occurs around two months, when the baby has achieved a certain degree of perceptual and cognitive development.

Because his mother's face is close enough, Billy can make eye contact. His hand is touching his mother's face tenderly and his mouth is pulled upward in enjoyment.

Love between parent and child may be hard to describe in words. Body language makes us feel both its presence and its absence.

Parents: Our First Love

Around the age of three, children become particularly attracted to the parent of the opposite sex. Their body language shows this clearly: they want to hug, kiss, and touch.

Amelia just adores her father. She is a lucky girl: she has a father who returns her love without being seductive.

Expressions of Love

The happy excitement that physical contact with their parents elicits from children of this age is shown by the body language of three-year-old Scott. His arm is in motion, as if fighting off overwhelming feelings.

Once safely past the upheaval and confusion that feelings of love and jealousy bring during the years from three to six or so, most children successfully identify with the parent of the same sex. Most experts emphasize that it is important to give children a great deal of tangible expression of love, even after they are no longer "babies."

Maya is nine years old in this photograph; she loves lazy mornings, when her mother allows her to come and cuddle with her. They express their closeness in harmonious, circular movements.

Love Between Brother and Sister

David is leaning toward his baby sister Laurie, who reaches toward him with her whole body, her hand, and her tongue. Even if you could not see the expression on the two children's faces, you would know by their gestures that they love each other.

This picture of four-year-old Lars gazing at his newborn sister Kristina so lovingly is not a "chance" photograph. More than any child I know, he demonstrated positive feelings toward Kristina from the start. I have many loving, harmonious pictures of them. In this photograph, his smile is tender, even amused, his arm supportive, with no sign of hostility in any part of his body. Both children are relaxed and comfortable.

Love of Pets

Loving a pet can be a wonderful preparation for loving and caring for another human being. Fortunately, the pets will tell you with their own body language if they feel mistreated by a child who is either too young or too aggressive to be allowed to have one.

Four-year-old Chip and his puppy are a joy to behold, rolling on the floor, cuddling, playing. They seem to have the same "smile" on their faces. Their movements also show an awareness of each other: neither is going to hurt the other.

When Chrissy, then five years old, came to visit my cat's four-week-old kittens, she immediately knew how to play with them. Her loving nature expresses itself through her movements: she is bending down to the kitten's level, encouraging those first, wobbly steps with both words and body language.

Maureen, six, is expressing her love to her puppy by crouching to get close to him, and embracing him without squeezing.

Love

Eric's parents immediately put this photograph up on their bulletin board. They found it a beautiful expression of love and tenderness between brother and sister. Their enjoyment of the picture—which could evoke uncomfortable feelings in some other parents—shows their relaxed attitude about sensual physical contact.

Sexual Feelings

In your mind, try for a moment to substitute grownups for the two children on these pages. Wouldn't you call what you see "sex play"?

Maya, five, and Ian, three, are sister and brother, brought up with as much freedom and respect for their true natures as is possible. They often run around naked and don't consider that anything to be ashamed of.

There are opposing views, though, about whether acting out everything that they feel will help or hinder their mature feelings.

6. JEALOUSY, AMBIVALENCE

Jealousy is one of the facts of family life.

Firstborns have to learn to share their parents with the newborns. Later, as unique relationships develop between each child and the parents, the inevitable differences will be keenly felt by the children. It is nearly inescapable that each will feel jealous of the other in varying degrees.

Even children who say little or nothing about these feelings will betray them through their body language.

Three-year-old Valerie is expressing her jealousy in subtle ways. First, she bites her lip; then she covers her mother's eyes: *that* should make baby disappear! What clearer message could she send through body language?

Acting Out Jealousy

To distract his mother from the baby, Christopher, three, has just told his
mother a funny story and asked her to tie his shoelaces. Now he is "playing"
with the baby. That the baby interprets this play as the aggressive action it
is can be seen from the startled expression around her mouth and the tension
in her hand.

Mother seems relaxed; I remember my reaction to this scene was that she
was perhaps a bit *too* relaxed. But, later in the day, she casually mentioned
that at the present time she wouldn't dream of leaving the two children
alone even for a minute. Evidently she had understood all the nonverbal
body language messages Christopher had sent her about his jealousy.

Two-year-olds rarely express their jealousy in words; they act it out, sometimes in more complicated ways than the preceding photographs have shown.

Chrissy, who had given up her own bottle, now picks up her baby sister's bottle any chance she gets, especially when her mother is tending the baby.

Like many other children in her situation, she has regressed to more babyish ways. Other children sometimes develop stuttering and bedwetting; they show a greater dependency when the new baby arrives.

A pattern of regression to the bottle, begun at this time, may continue to be one source of a lifelong syndrome of overeating and overdrinking.

Sibling Rivalry

Six-year-old Adam expresses his jealousy both verbally and nonverbally, through body language. After watching his mother bathe and dress baby Peter, he suddenly crept under the baby's crib and declared: "I am in baby's jail now."

In this case, body language is expressed by *where* he went (under the crib, into an imagined jail). What a powerful message, how appropriate to what he felt!

Being a middle child is recognized as a precarious position in the family constellation. The oldest has a special place, and so does a new baby: the middle child is jealous of both. He alternately wants the privileges and responsibilities of his older sibling *and* the attention the new baby gets.

After Billy, seven, was given the job of comforting baby Kevin, four-year-old Robert, the middle child, sits near them sunk in jealousy. He stares unblinking. He pushes his mouth down, hunches his shoulders and comforts himself with his hand.

Billy, who has had to live with his jealousy of Robert in past years, now gets back at him by emphasizing his new privileges with the baby. He is excluding his younger brother by the way he is holding the baby away from him.

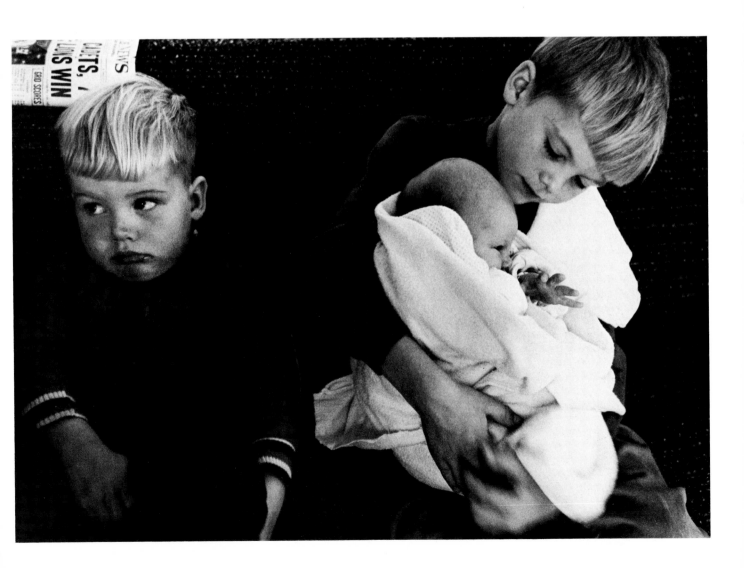

Ambivalence Toward the New Baby

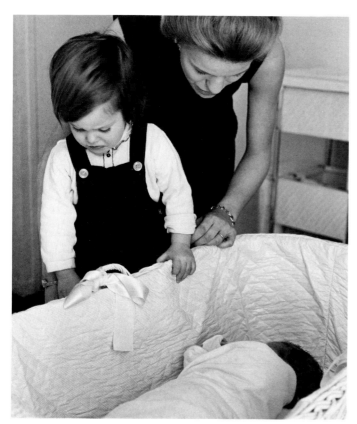 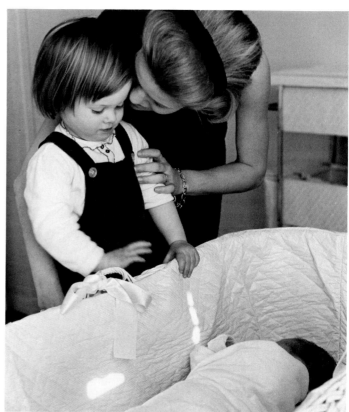

Mother has just come home from the hospital with the new baby. Two-year-old Minty has been looking forward to this moment; yet, when Mother asks whether she would like to see the baby installed in Minty's old bassinette, she says "yes" but looks as if she had said "no."

In the first photograph, we see her glance away, a look of distress on her face. In the second, she is still looking down, listening to her mother's words of endearment. Her right hand is in motion, as if waving "go away!" or "take her away!"

In the third photograph, Mother's words have aroused her curiosity; she is ready to touch the newcomer. She is moving her hand back and forth tentatively.

By now, the baby is awake. Minty retreats from

her perch, expressing her ambivalence by looking friendly but biting the edge of the bassinette. In the last photograph, her mother is holding her hand tenderly, and Minty is at last willing to touch the baby. She is delighted when little Melissa grabs her fingers.

Perhaps it could be fun to have a baby around?

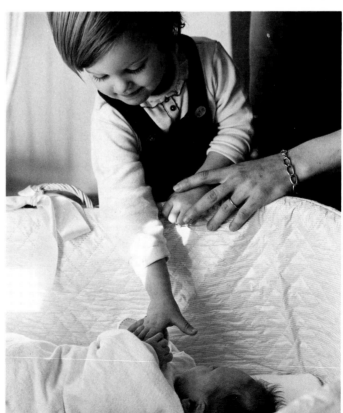

7. HOSTILITY

Whether we like it or not, hostility is a part of our emotional makeup. No baby can be brought up without frustrations; and frustrations breed negative, angry feelings. While it is an unhealthy and unhappy child who is constantly hostile, it is natural that negative feelings will occur in even the most loved and loving child.

Anger is being expressed when eyes narrow, brows contract, mouths turn downward, and hands are raised menacingly.

Dolls: Substitute Targets

Dolls are an easy and safe target for a child's hostility; this is one of the reasons why many experts today encourage children of both sexes to play with them.

I didn't observe any preliminary to eighteen-month-old Carole's picking up the doll she was playing with and biting it with all her strength. Her facial expression is noncommittal, devoid of real anger, and her hands are holding the doll normally. The only clue to the reason for the biting is in her eyes: they are looking intently in the direction of her mother, who is sitting, occupied in her own work.

At age four, Maureen is full of reproaches while playing with her favorite doll. "Bad girl! Didn't I tell you to keep out of the dirt? Now what shall I do with you?" And so it goes.

We should not jump to the conclusion that Maureen is just imitating her mother; she is probably inventing her own play, to get rid of hostility.

Terry, age six, is being scolded by her mother. She is a timid, rather shy child, so she just puckers her mouth and takes it. But wait: what is her right arm doing? Moving slightly, is her hand in a fist? It looks as if she wants to hit something, or maybe someone.

She finishes dressing her doll, and then, all of a sudden, she starts spanking it. If her expression is any guide, then parents who used to say, "This hurts me more than it hurts you," while punishing their children, may have spoken the truth. Terry looks unhappy: her eyebrows knotted, her mouth compressed.

Again: we should not draw the conclusion that Terry is habitually spanked herself; researchers have reported that even children who were never spanked take out their hostility on dolls and other children by hitting them.

Anger, Contempt

I am often asked to take a photograph of two or more children together. I know that I am meant to produce a shot in which brothers and sisters sit or stand close together, smiling sweetly. This fantasy picture rarely comes off, so I show the parents what other things are going on in the photograph, consoling them by pointing out that in the years to come, this true-to-life picture will evoke more accurate memories than any successfully posed one.

I had just managed to support the baby in three-year-old Elisabeth's arms for a nice double portrait; but before I could take even one shot, Elisabeth grabbed the pacifier from the baby's hand. Now she is exulting in ferocious glee.

Poor baby: she is just starting to understand that her pacifier is gone from her still-grasping hand. She is opening her eyes and mouth wide in surprise. Elisabeth's brow is furrowed, her eyebrows pulled together, and her nose pulled upward; this is usually a sign of disgust or contempt and makes for a most unusual expression in such a young child.

Morgan, four, is painting Easter eggs. His neighbor has finished hers and is now expressing what she thinks of Morgan's efforts by lifting her shoulder, pulling her mouth downward while at the same time pushing her nose and chin slightly upward.

I tried to imitate this complicated body language in front of a mirror. It is an amazingly good way to express contempt. Pulling one's mouth downward only conveys sadness; all the other muscles are needed to add up to the disdain evident in the picture.

Physical Expression of Hostility

This is the only photograph I ever took of a child hitting his parent. The mother's surprise is visible: she flinches with closed eyes, her mouth in the "ooh" position of pain. Two-year-old Johnny's face reflects not only the anger and frustration he felt when he was told that he had to go to bed, but also his unhappiness over what he just did. His left hand is pointing accusingly at his mother, but his mouth and brow look as if he is going to start crying at any moment.

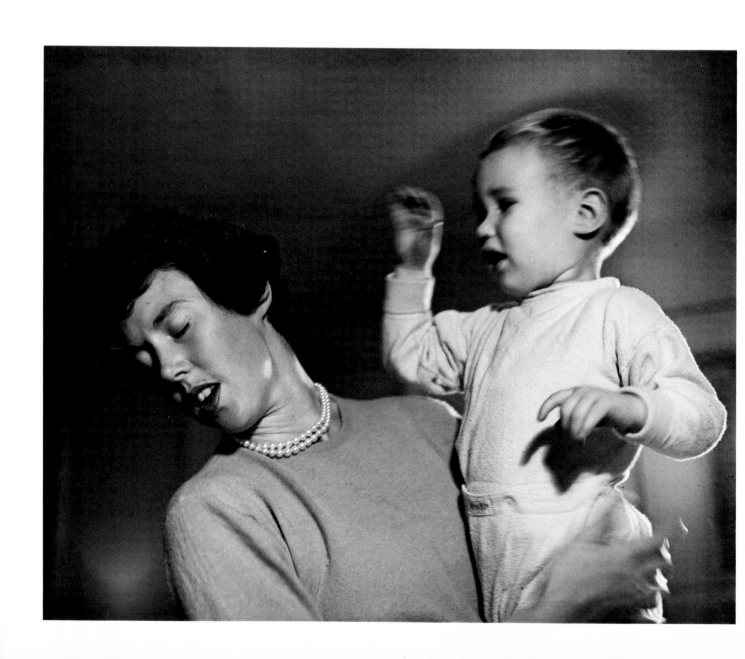

I was too far away to hear what the argument between John and David was, but their body language makes it easy to guess. Six-year-old David is clinging to his tricycle, refusing to move; John, eight, is threatening him in a classic pose of challenge and superiority. His right arm is lifted, palms up, his hands in a fist; he is showing off his strength and his willingness to fight.

This scene reminds me of animals establishing their physical superiority with similar body language: cats arching their backs, dogs baring teeth. Most of the time, the weaker one makes himself even smaller and concedes the ground to the stronger one without a fight.

I often observe how much importance children attach to the word "MINE!" They may have dozens of toys, but let another child approach their tricycle and war breaks out immediately.

This kind of possessiveness actually represents a positive stage of development, not merely greed. A child who is beginning to recognize his separate individuality and positive image of himself will feel very threatened by any attack on his possessions. Sharing usually develops only after a child has a basic sense of trust.

Johnny, four, and Gerry, three, are both holding on to the tricycle with all their force and attacking each other by pulling, kicking, and yelling. The explicitness of their body language shows that this is no joking matter to them.

Fighting Over Possessions

Christmas is supposed to be the feast of joy and love, but ask any parent and you will hear many tales: of expectations that are so high that no reality can satisfy them; of children wanting only what the others received; of fights breaking out right under the Christmas tree. It is hard to explain to a two-year-old that he cannot handle the same toys as his four-year-old brother.

One marble is the cause of the fight between five-year-old identical twins Andrew and Jonathan. Their parents have decided to cut down on fights by buying two of everything; this photograph shows that the children will still find something to battle over.

Birthdays can be another source of frustration. Children like to get presents, but they have a hard time letting their friends play with them. Susie, four, is one of the children who gets upset if her possessions are being used by other children. Her wide-open mouth, narrowed eyes, and knitted brows show how angry she is. Billy is holding on to the toy car grimly. His mouth is pursed, his eyebrows are lowered; his whole attitude is unyielding and furious.

8. UNHAPPINESS

The jealous, aggressive, and fearful children we have been looking at in the previous chapter are unhappy most of the time. In this section, we are examining other, less permanent reasons for unhappiness: physical discomfort, pain, not getting what one wants right away; not feeling secure enough; and being bored.

Feeling Sick

The *only* way that babies can tell us they are unhappy is through their body language, including crying. They wrinkle their foreheads, draw their eyebrows together, let their mouth hang open or turn downward, hunch their shoulders, draw their hands into fists, and tense all their muscles. Even if only one or two of these expressions of unhappiness are present, parents learn to understand their children's "language."

Six-week-old David is feeling uncomfortable. His mother, reading his body language signals correctly, knows that he must be getting a cold and is giving him lots of attention and cuddling. Only babies who feel that the world is a place where people are aware of their needs will be able to develop trust later. This is a critically important step in avoiding much unhappiness throughout life.

Unfulfilled Wish

Young children live in the present moment; it takes a while before they learn concepts like "soon," "later," or "not now." Looking at three-and-a-half-year-old Maya's unhappy face, we can see that she thinks she will always feel miserable. The truth is that she couldn't get something she wanted right then and there. But she soon forgot her unhappiness.

It took me a while to understand that one has to consider the *prevalence* of happiness or unhappiness, in order to know how to assess a child's state of well-being.

Both feelings often coexist, turning laughter into tears and unhappiness into happiness within seconds.

Temporary and Lasting Unhappiness

Elisabeth, three, is on her way upstairs to get away from the picture-taking session. She is trailing her security blanket behind her. It not only comforts her but also serves as a way to attract attention. To judge by her downturned mouth and wrinkled brow, she does not feel very good about the world right now.

Two-year-old Allison is reacting strongly to some recent changes in her family's situation. She often pushes out her lower lip, pulls down the corners of her mouth and stares into space for long moments, as if thinking hard.

While a photograph can show only one second of expression, in reality the mood can be either fleeting or lasting. Allison's pained expression is anything but fleeting; she is going through a difficult time, brought about by her parents' imminent divorce, which she must have sensed partly by their changed body language toward each other.

Thumbsucking

Thumbsucking is widely interpreted as a gesture of insecurity and even unhappiness. It bothers some parents, but others regard it only as a satisfaction of the sucking instinct, stronger in some children than in others.

Thumbsucking can also be a sign of hunger in babies, another instance of body language giving parents valuable clues.

Mary Beth, four, sucks her thumb when she is tired. Then she likes to retreat into herself, her eyes dreamy. Her parents know this sign by now and try to persuade her to take a nap when she looks like this.

Repressed Anger

Six-year-old Adam's eyes have the staring, unblinking quality that we associate with unhappiness. He is looking past the photographer at his family. His left hand is tense, with the index finger extended in accusation.

It wasn't hard to discover the source of his unhappiness. He was six years old when his little brother was born, too old to vent his negative, jealous feelings as easily as a two- or three-year-old could have done. It took him quite a while to overcome his unhappiness.

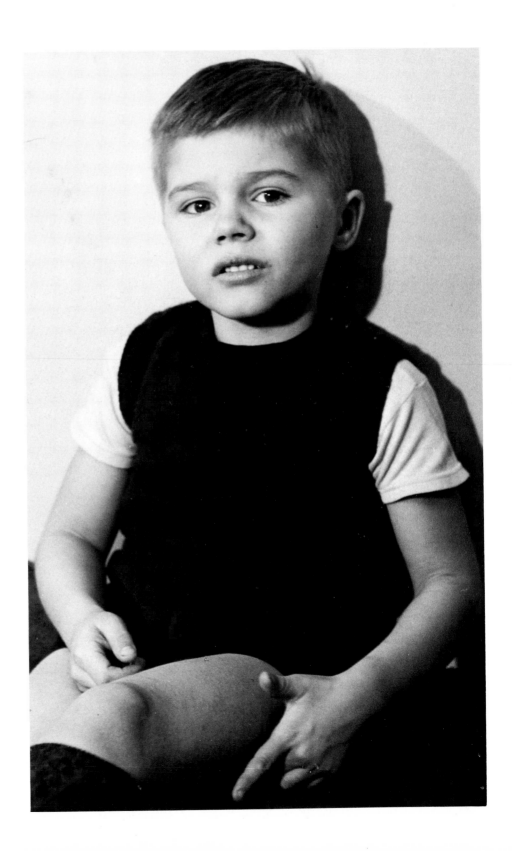

Unhappiness Caused by Pain

Even after children learn to speak, their body language can be a valuable clue in many situations. Suppose they take a fall and come in, crying so hard that one cannot understand clearly what they are trying to say. Their expressions should be a reliable guide to the extent of their injury. Are they walking normally, or are their muscles limp? Do their eyes focus?

In the case of six-year-old Alexandra, one has to take into consideration that she is an extremely expressive child; her body language is probably exaggerated. A little hugging and comforting, two band-aids, and she will be off playing again.

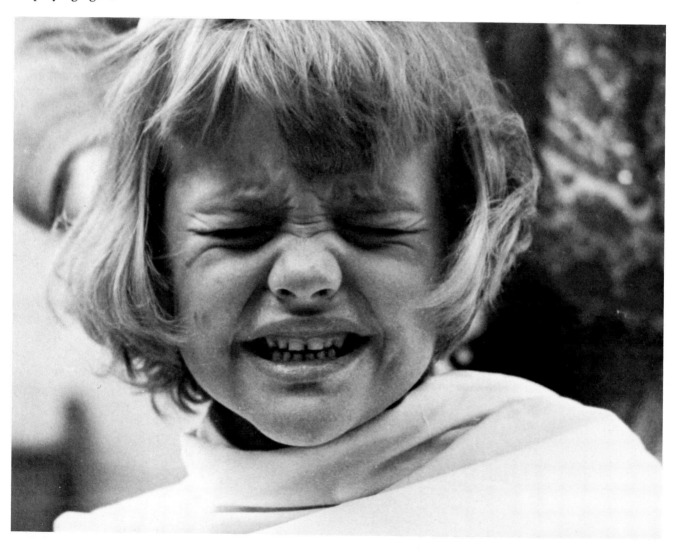

And how about three-year-old Chrissy? All she is saying to her mother is "Mummy! Mummy!" which is not much enlightenment to an anxious parent who comes running. Looking at her closely, we notice that though she has been crying bitterly, there are more tears on her chin than near her eyes, which means that she has stopped crying.

She is sitting in a normal position, leaning on a hassock in a fairly relaxed manner. Mother can go back to her work after a few kisses.

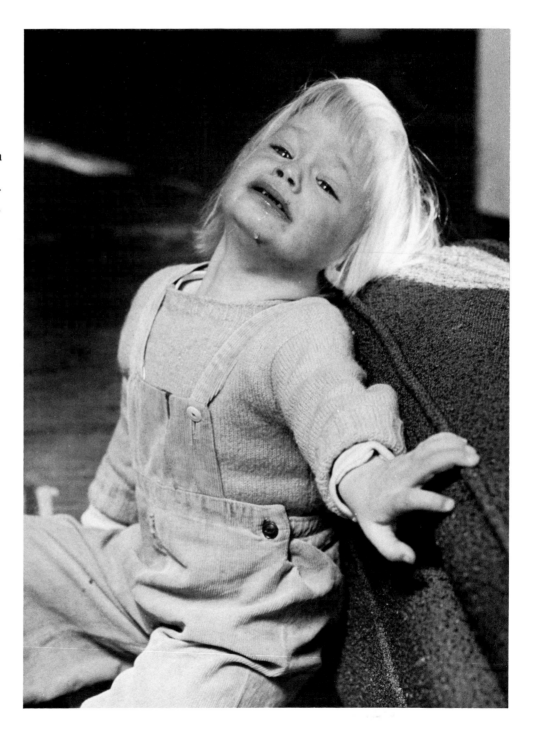

Punishment

Peter, age five, has been confined to his room as
punishment. His face is slack in discouragement; he
seems to be one of those sensitive children to whom
this isolation—however short—is hard to take. He
looks downcast, a word which relies on body language
to convey its meaning.

Six-year-old Morgan is expressing his boredom by slouching in an armchair, peculiarly quiet and serious. He is picking at the skin of one hand with the other.

Unhappiness often expresses itself in similar movements: pulling at a lock of hair, picking at the nose, or scratching a scab until it bleeds.

Maureen, eight, finds herself at home with no one to play with. She cannot think of anything that she would like to do and she says she is bored. She is biting her lip and staring straight ahead, unblinking. Her left hand seems to give the clue to her feelings: it is turned palm upwards, which usually denotes that she is begging for someone to give her something; that she feels empty and needy.

Exclusion

Body language is often used consciously or unconsciously by two or more people to exclude others. They turn their backs, form a closed triangle with their legs, or lean toward each other and away from the excluded person.

The next two photographs show children being excluded in obvious ways.

Just a few moments before, four-year-old Darrell was happy to be included in the job of picking apples. Now she feels upset, alone, and ignored. Her two older friends are sharing secrets and excluding her by leaning toward each other and away from her. Darrell hunches her shoulders in her unhappiness, turns her mouth downward and stares.

Begging to Be Accepted

It is hard for a child who has known much trouble and rejection in his short life to trust people.

When Bobby, aged eight, sees a group absorbed in what his counselor is showing them, he stops a few yards away instead of joining them. They fail to notice him and so he just stands there, longing to be with them. His right hand, especially, speaks volumes: it is extended, palm upward, in the classic posture of beggars. "Please . . . give me . . ." it seems to say.

9. HAPPINESS

Nearly all children are born with the potential to be happy. Their early experiences, especially with love and security, make them capable of continuing being happy to a greater or lesser degree.

There are numerous causes of happiness for children: love, food, sensual delights like sand and water, movement, friends. Whatever the cause, children's happiness is expressed in practically identical body language.

Most happy children smile; all seem to be very loose in their movements, in motion without hurry. The open mouths curve upward, the brows clear, the pupil of the eyes often dilated. The body language of happiness is also the *absence* of the signs that characterize unhappiness.

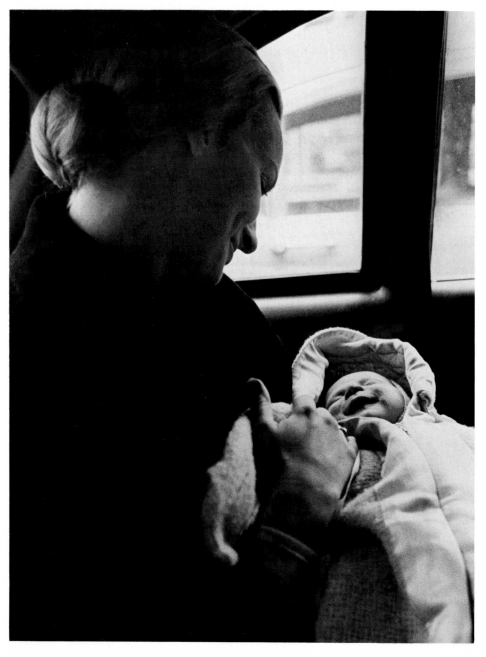

Edward is only five days old and on his way home from the hospital where he was born. He is evidently enjoying being jiggled in the car and being held by his mother. His beatific expression lasted so long that I believe it reflected good feelings of comfort and relaxation, not just so-called "gas-pain."

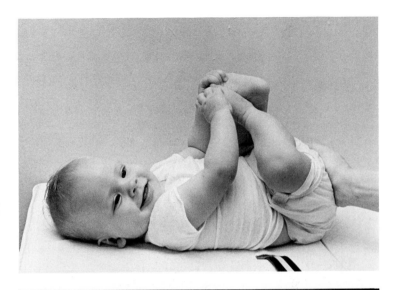

Six-month-old Billy has just been diapered and now he is playing with his recently discovered toes. His rounded cheeks, upward-curling mouth, and relaxed body radiate contentment.

In the first few months of life, babies cannot move their bodies from one place to another by themselves. No wonder they find so much pleasure in moving around as their motor development progresses.

Cindy is reveling in her new-found freedom of movement: at nine months of age, she has just learned to crawl.

Cindy's smile is pushing her cheeks upward, making them look round and full. Maybe that's why we associate roundness with happiness, while drawn, downward movements signify unhappiness.

Water Is Happiness

Nearly all children adore playing with water. Whether it is found in bathtub or kitchen sink, puddle or pond, pouring rain or mighty ocean, children want to touch it, drink it, wallow in it.

Sarah, left, and Adam, opposite, love their baths and would like to spend hours playing in the water. They laugh, smile, and splash.

Below, nine-month-old Adam doesn't stop his toothless grin for a moment while he is exploring the warm sand at the beach, letting it run between his fingers and cling deliciously to his body.

Seven-year-old Kim has ventured into the swirling waves of the ocean; she lets the water tickle and caress her, the feeling of danger adding to her enjoyment.

Other children may need help in overcoming their fear of water, but it is worth the effort. Playing in water and sand is a joy that they express with every muscle of their bodies.

Happiness, Gaiety

Eating makes eighteen-month-old Morgan happy; and why shouldn't it? Food is delicious and he is neither too thin nor too fat.

Parents used to worry whether their babies were sufficiently "fat and healthy." Now it seems to be generally accepted that fat is *not* synonymous with healthy and fat children are likely to grow up into fat adults. Today most parents concern themselves about a child whose delight in eating seems out of proportion and who wants to be consoled with food for every setback.

Lars, four, is playing on his jungle gym and I am perched on a chair, taking his picture. All of a sudden, the chair tilts and I start to fall off. Luckily, I manage to hold on and catch the glee in Lars's eyes. He thinks I looked really funny and bursts out laughing.

In German, there is a wonderful word: *Schadenfreude*, meaning happiness over someone else's misfortune. It is such a common source of humor that it seems strange that some languages lack this word. For instance, what else makes people laugh at slapstick?

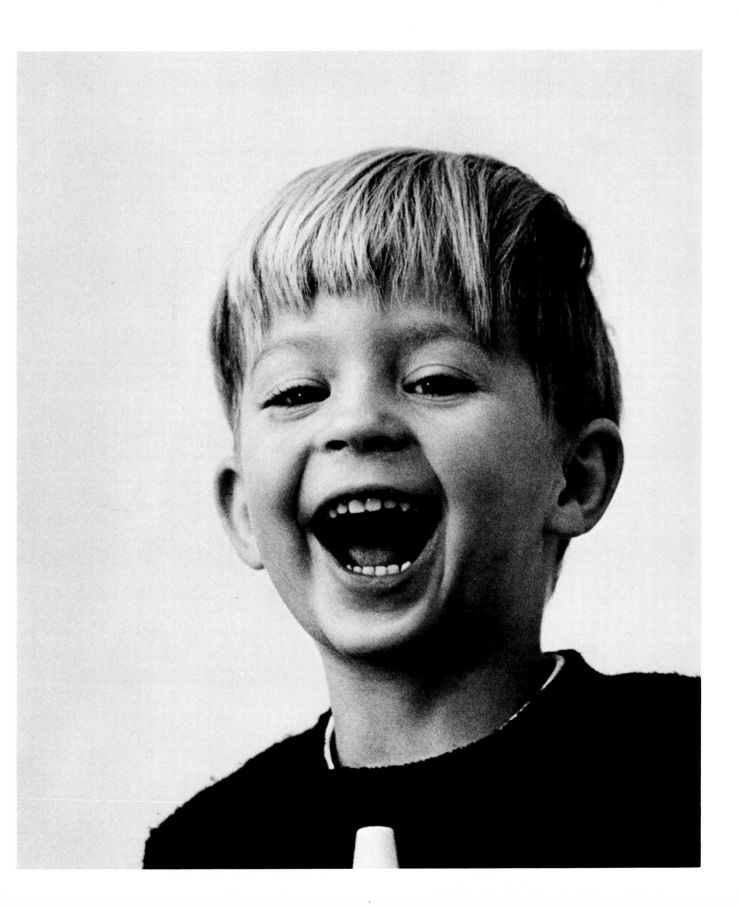

Happiness Is a New Dress—or None at All

Four-year-old Chrissy, like many children, runs around in blue jeans all day. She likes to see and handle her mother's pretty clothes, but this photograph captures the first time that she gets really excited about a new dress of her own. She is brushing her hair to make the transformation perfect, admiring herself in the mirror.

Her posture is still that of a "tomboy" used to pants, but the look in her eyes acknowledges that it is nice to look beautiful.

Chrissy was overjoyed by a beautiful dress—but three-year-old Jenny is made happy by taking hers off. I had been photographing her perched on the rocking horse; when I said, "We're finished, so you can take your Sunday dress off," she proceeded to take *all* her clothes off, enjoying the freedom of running around naked, letting the air bathe her body.

She seems to be weightless, her feet hardly touching the ground, all muscles working harmoniously, her hair flying.

She is happy to be doing something that is usually forbidden. At her age, she is already expected to be "modest" and wear a bathing suit to the beach.

Laughter

Sometimes it looks as if the mere act of moving around made children happy. Running, bicycling, flying through the air in Father's arms or in a swing— all activity makes them laugh joyfully.

Sarah, four, is one of these children, always on the move, the faster the better. She is swooshing through the air on her swing, feeling alternately scared and exhilarated.

Her face is hard to describe: closed eyes and closed but widely pulled lips don't sound as if they belonged to the body language of happiness. But there are added muscles at work, pulling all lines upward, which make her face look ecstatic.

Chrissy, six, and Margaretta, four, are taking a boatride around Manhattan; they have stopped at a place where the wind blows their skirts high. They think this is a wonderful sensation and they giggle excitedly.

Their mouths are pulled sideways as far as possible; they squint their eyes, huddling together. Such spontaneous, happy moments crop up in most sisters' and brothers' lives and counterbalance the problems of sibling rivalry.

Letting Go

All children feel a conflict between wanting to mess around and learning to be tidy and clean. Five-year-old Marina is nearly hysterical with happiness about having smeared herself with paint while making Easter eggs in her family's Russian tradition.

To give vent to similar feelings, most nurseries and schools encourage finger-painting and sand- and water-play. It is amazing to discover that quite a few children in each class don't *dare* to get messy. When they finally allow themselves the tactile sensation of using paints, glue, and water, their reactions often match the one Marina shows in this photograph.

The expression on Laurie's and Bobby's faces, happily jumping on a bed, is a strong argument for giving children a chance to participate in gymnastics and sports in which they can move vigorously. There is an elation felt in the body and the mind after a good workout that is a strong positive influence on lifelong good health.

Happiness is contagious when people dance, whether they are children or adults. Observe the faces of any folk dancing group, for instance: eyes sparkle, mouths are half-open, and cheeks are rounded. All look happy from the sheer pleasure of moving with the music.

This seven-year-old girl is dancing to a record, acting out the story it tells about cowboys.

10. THE JOYS OF ACHIEVEMENT

Physical Achievements

In this chapter, the photographs show how children express their pleasure in successfully mastering their bodies, learning something, making something, or doing something.

Receiving appreciation and recognition at each step of achievement encourages children to try out new skills. Most parents are well aware of this process and applaud their children's first efforts. Ideally, the whole educational process would consist of motivating children to learn more and more difficult tasks.

The photographs on these two pages show us children all aglow over their first efforts to master a physical feat.

Sarah, at a mere two months of age, can now raise her head while lying on her stomach. It must be wonderful for babies to develop a measure of control over where they can look. After they can turn over by themselves, this freedom increases.

By the age of nine months, Margaretta has learned to crawl and doesn't want to be confined to a playpen any longer. Her mother lets her creep around, even though Margaretta now requires more constant supervision. The happiness on her daughter's shining face rewards her for her extra work.

Kristina and Mary, both one-year-olds, are learning to walk, holding on to their mother's hands or to thin air for support. Their joy over this new achievement is visible in their smiles, sparkling eyes, and harmonious muscle coordination.

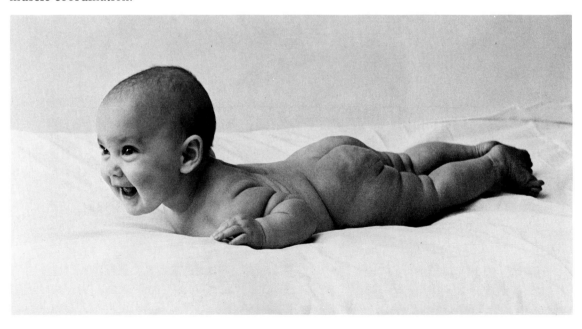

New Achievements

Two-and-a-half-year-old Minty has just put on her left shoe *all by herself*. Not until you have tried to direct someone to follow all the steps that are necessary to accomplish this seemingly simple task can you appreciate all the skill and perseverance it requires.

The great educator Maria Montessori worked out step by step directions for teaching a child to open and close a door, put on shoes and clothes, button buttons, and zip zippers.

Children sometimes get frustrated when a grownup cannot explain the ways to perform a task because they never before considered its complexity.

I have often heard children say, "I must finish my work," when they were really talking about their play. After all, play *is* children's work; and, if properly presented, work can become play. Painting is fun whether one messes around with fingerpaints or learns to cover a wall with paint. Simple cooking, decorating a cake, or scrubbing a table clean can give lots of pleasure.

While at summer camp, six-year-old Jennifer is enjoying her daily job of sweeping the pavilion where they will dance and play later.

Nat, age two, has often seen his older brother play with a toy that goes round and round when pushed in a certain way. Until now, Nat was unable to do it himself. Under the watchful eye of his brother (who doesn't want to see his toy damaged) and his father, who is giving detailed directions, Nat has finally made it work.

His elation is visible not only in his smiling, upward-turned face, but also in the position of his left hand. The moment the toy started to spin, a tense fist became a spread-open "star". This is a movement often used by magicians after they perform a trick, as if announcing: "Here: I have done it!"

Artistic Accomplishments

Involvement in artistic pursuits puts a special glow on the faces of children. While they dedicate themselves to their tasks, their bodies are limber, working harmoniously. They radiate a self-confidence that must color their lives at other times too.

Primitive dances and rhythmic accompaniment were among the earliest instances of communication through body language.

Four-year-old Robin is the son of two musicians. He has been singing, dancing, and playing simple instruments since he was very small. He also likes to make up and act out his own songs while accompanying himself on a drum.

Alexandra is learning to dance at school. Dancing around without rules can be lots of fun too, but there is special fascination in following very precise and exacting instructions and being able to do the dances correctly. It instills discipline and shows that there is a particular satisfaction in mastering something demanding.

Creative Achievements

Alison, four, is holding on to the chair with her feet like a little monkey, so her whole body can participate in the creation of her painting.

Five-year-old Olivia's face is shining with pleasure while she is painting. Maybe that's not just a metaphor: skin does get tauter when cheeks are pushing upward in a wide smile, and reflect more light that way.

Peach, seven, is showing her involvement with her creative work by leaning toward it in total dedication. She is taking part in an afternoon art course held by the Museum of Modern Art in New York. She wishes she could go there every day.

The Joy of Learning

Few classrooms present a more harmonious scene than one in which children are taught by the Montessori method. Maria Montessori recognized that children don't have to be forced to learn: that, given beautiful and exciting "toys," they will beg for the chance to work a few minutes longer rather than going outside for recess.

All the children on these pages show their absorption and pleasure in the way they lean toward their work, use their hands, and talk to themselves in order to solve problems that would often baffle adults.

Leslie is only four years old, but all of a sudden he has discovered that he can read! Because he is attending a school in which pupils are allowed to move about freely, he is spending the whole morning showing off his new-found skill to one child after another.

The ability to read often comes before the child has learned to write. So the introduction of typewriters into schools, from first grade on, has proved to be a shortcut for many children. Six-year-old Selena's enjoyment in using the typewriter is apparent in her wide smile, her eager hands, and her leaning toward her work.

This five-year-old is using her mind to the fullest, as she grapples with a complicated mathematical problem. Her mouth is pursed in concentration. Her lower lip is sucked in, a movement indicating her wish to be very careful. Her brow and left hand are relaxed, showing her confidence in what she is doing. Her right hand approaches the blocks she is using in her work with delicacy and precision.

Ruby, eight, has made herself at home in the classroom by removing her shoes. She is concentrating on her lesson. Were she to tap her hands or feet, doodle, whistle, or lean away from her work, we would read her body language signs differently and understand that she was *not* interested in what she was doing.

School Achievements

Chrissy, now grown up to be a third-grader, is coming out of school and is approaching her mother, who has come to pick her up. Can Mother tell whether Chrissy has had a good day at school? I think she can, if she understands her daughter's body language.

If she were smiling only because she is glad school is over, Chrissy would hardly be carrying her books on top of her head in the manner in which peasants transport their possessions. A child unhappy with school would carry her books casually, even carelessly.

Seven-year-old Kim has just walked in after school, and even though her
mother has been doing something else, she immediately focuses her attention
on what her daughter wants to show her. Mother shows herself to be properly
impressed by the neat writing exercise, so Kim is beaming with pleasure.

Mother's words of praise and encouragement are reinforced by the way
she is leaning toward her daughter and by the way she is holding the piece
of paper gently and respectfully.

III
The Effect of Parents' Body Language on Children

1. PRE-VERBAL LEARNING FROM PARENTS

Children's actions and body language communications are determined partly by inborn factors (thumbsucking, for instance); partly by imitation (pattycake); and partly by direct teaching ("sit up straight!").

Parents play an important role in affecting which factors will dominate.

Before babies come to understand spoken language, their actions and interactions are strongly influenced by their parents' body language. Babies will reciprocate a smile or start to fuss when they sense that the parent who is holding them is tense.

It is parents whom children most often imitate in their movements, mannerisms, expressions. In short: they learn their own body language from their parents.

Parents communicate their own true, uncensored feelings to their children through their—sometimes involuntary—body language.

The photographs on the following pages will clarify these observations.

Babies need human contact and stimulation through body language and talk. This process is so important that it is considered to be the main reason why babies in institutions suffer serious damage. They are deprived of enough contact with one caring adult who could transmit to them the feelings of love, security, and encouragement.

Dr. René Spitz, in his studies done in well-run institutions, has shown the extent of this damage most clearly. The babies he studied learned much less, much later. They hardly knew how to smile, and a shocking percentage of them died of simple childhood illnesses—all because of the lack of affectionate human contact.

On the other hand, Dr. Spitz found that a healthy baby will respond to an adult's smile reinforced by nodding.

This mother is smiling and nodding to her three-month-old baby, who is responding with glee.

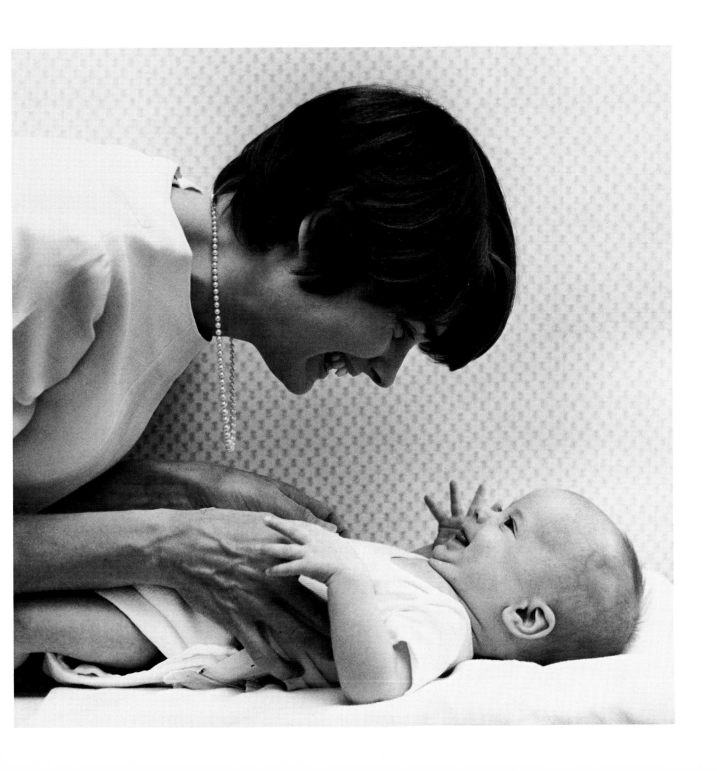

Communicating with a Pre-Verbal Child

If you have ever completely lost your voice to laryngitis, you will recall how much you were able to communicate by sign and body language alone. Small children are experts at understanding their parents' thoughts, wishes, and commands, even without language.

Parents who take it for granted that their small children "understand" everything they tell them do the babies a great service, because, as they talk, their body language communicates a lot to the young. Most will respond from their infancy on by making sounds, gurgling, and generally sounding as if they were answering their parents.

David is only ten days old in this photograph, but he is behaving as if he were conducting an intelligent conversation with his mother.

Outstretched arms mean: "Come here!" and children try to reach those arms as soon as they are able to. One-year-old Jeannot extends his hand to reach toward his mother.

Six-month-old Billy likes to listen while his father sings and accompanies himself on the guitar. He tries to sing along too, much the way cats and dogs sometimes make sounds when they hear singing or sounds coming from different instruments.

2. LEARNING BY IMITATION

It is important to remember how much children learn in the first year of their lives: more than they will ever learn in any other year of their life. Most of it happens by imitation, guesswork, and by reading their parents' body language. It all seems to be a game, but actually it is a complicated and important learning process.

All four of these young children are imitating their parents; clapping their hands, waving bye-bye, showing how big they are, throwing kisses. While the parents act out these movements, they usually also say what they mean. This repeated association of words and body language *is* the way a child eventually learns to talk.

Teaching by Demonstration

As children learn to talk, one of their first expressions is likely to be "ME TOO!" Sometimes they will say "Johnny do it!" or simply "Johnny," said with upstretched arms.

They want to do everything they see others do. Two-year-old Johnny likes to "play piano" with his mother—the best way to learn.

It is fun to watch mothers feeding their young children. Most of them
unconsciously move their lips, open their mouth, and swallow
imaginary food in order to encourage the children to do the same.

Imitating Parents

For most people the first years of their lives remain hidden from memory. Parents have a chance to re-experience these years through their children. When the children pick up their mannerisms and body language, it becomes doubly fascinating. Grandparents often comment on the similarity between the behavior of their children when they were little and the way the grandchildren act now.

Two-year-old Billy cannot see his father's expressions as he sits on his shoulders. Still, in photograph after photograph, his inherited and learned movements mirror his father's.

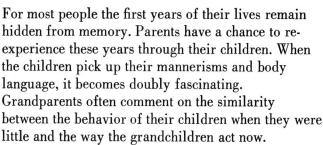

Children start imitative play at an early age. "I'll be the mummy and you be the baby," they say as they play at feeding and dressing each other. They also like to dress up in adult clothes and act out their parents' roles. They usually imitate the parent of the same sex, but in this photograph Maureen, five, has put on Daddy's jacket and Tommy, seven, Mummy's old feathered hat and long dress.

Pretending to Be Mother

Stacey had an interesting idea for her twelfth birthday party: she asked all her girlfriends to come dressed as their own mothers. Inspired by their make-up, elegant dresses, and high heels, the girls did more than *look* like their mothers: they also *acted* out a fantasy of adult behavior. They smoked, they drank a lot. They used their hands in insincere and pretentious gestures. Their conversation centered around excuses for not accepting invitations, descriptions of their new acquisitions, and complaints about their children.

As I knew some of the mothers personally, I didn't take any of this to be an accurate depiction of reality. Still, I wondered what elements of reality went into the charade they played out.

Identifying with a Male or Female Model

In his book *Raising Children in a Difficult Time*, Dr. Benjamin Spock writes: "Most psychiatrists have assumed in the past that a definite sexual identity—knowing clearly that you are male or female—is a vital element in mental health." But he adds that *he* has come to believe that the definition of sexual identity does not need to be based on an emphasis of differences in clothing or playthings, or on parental reminders of what little boys are meant to do and what little girls are meant to do.

It is natural that five-year-old Howard should learn from his father how to put on a tie, while Maria, four, imitates her aunt in the art of putting on lipstick.

These two photographs show the extent to which the children identify with the parent of the same sex. They move their mouths and other features in conformity with what they see the grownups doing.

Nontraditional Sex Role Behavior

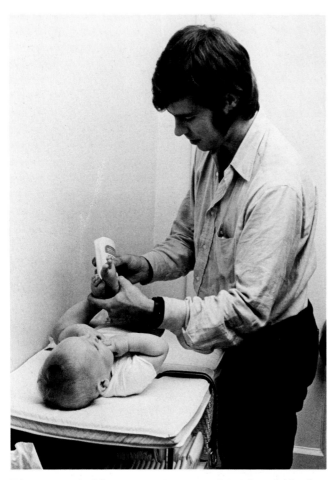

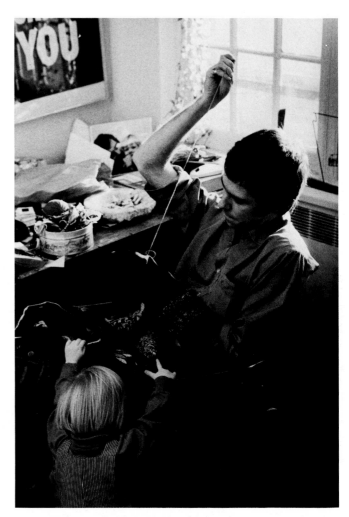

The women's liberation movement has already had a deep and lasting effect on what the children of today are taught. There were—and sometimes still are—many subtle ways in which boys are treated differently from girls. Boys are praised for *doing,* girls for being pretty. Children often see their mothers stay home and do all the housework, while father is rarely at home, but off somewhere earning a living. This can only work to the detriment of both boys and girls, forcing them into extremes of behavior, instead of letting them choose the elements of roles that suit them best individually.

Nat's view of the world of men and women will certainly be different from the clichés of yesterday. He sees his father share both baby care and household work with his mother. As often as not, he will go to his father when he needs something. He can also observe his father doing beautiful embroidery work as a hobby.

Most importantly, he is growing up in a household where equality and partnership are not mere words but an everyday reality.

Six-year-old Chris has fallen and hurt himself; his
teacher's body language, as she is comforting him, is
telling him that she sympathizes with him and that it
is perfectly all right for a boy to cry when he feels
like it.

Sex Role Similarities

When I heard of a school that is making a special effort to treat girls and boys equally, I asked for permission to document their work. I spent several days at the Woodward School in Brooklyn, N.Y., photographing boys and girls cooking and baking, playing with dolls, sharing cleanup work, doing carpentry together one hour and sewing the next. Boys were proud of the pretzels they baked. Girls wrote and acted out a play in which they cast themselves as astronauts. It seemed so natural, it was hard to remember that recently all these activities were segregated by sex.

I was especially interested in the school's efforts to involve both boys and girls in block-building, a play activity heretofore reserved for boys. It is also supposed to show up sex differences in the way children build: boys piling up tall phallic towers and girls laying out lower structures which they like to decorate by putting things inside.

Still, this is what I photographed the children doing. It remains to be seen whether the structures made by the two sexes will start to resemble each other more, now that boys and girls work and play together with equal expectations on the part of parents and teachers.

3. HOW CHILDREN REACT TO THEIR PARENTS' BODY LANGUAGE

One of my favorite *New Yorker* cartoons shows a man complaining to a young lady: "My problem is that my wife understands me." Well, maybe the problem of some parents is that their children understand them all too well.

The children develop this uncanny aptitude by being very sensitive to their parents' body language from the day they are born. Everyone knows stories of babies who can't sleep when their mothers are upset or of four-year-olds who start to misbehave when their parents are having marital problems which they thought were well hidden from the child.

While the grownups are having a short but heated argument, four-month-old Amy is getting more and more tense. Her eyebrows are pulled up in surprise and worry; she is staring rigidly and her mouth is turned down sharply. Her left hand forms a fist. No one could say that she is not conscious of and affected by the events and atmosphere around her.

Eighteen-month-old Christopher is observing curiously as his father is kissing his mother a tender goodbye. There is just a hint of tension in the way he holds his head, and, if you look carefully, you can see that his right hand is resting on his mother's bosom almost possessively. He would like to be part of the cuddle.

Nonverbal Communication

This mother was honest about her anger and frustration, and the children sensed it. So when she said, "Enough! I can't take another minute of this!" they soon stopped fighting and screaming.

Most psychologists agree that to be "nice" while seething inside is not only difficult but pointless. Children are experts at understanding body language and spotting hypocrisy. It is much better if children learn that grownups are honest and say what they communicate to them anyway in many subtle ways.

There are innumerable small body language signals. For instance, some parents allow their children to climb a tree but don't stop frowning; others tell their children, "Take your time!" but keep tapping their foot. Or they may say, "I don't mind that your report card is bad"—but they lean away from the child and avoid touching him or her. They might as well say what they really feel and stop giving contradictory information to their children, creating confusion and anxiety in them.

On the day they brought home the new baby from the hospital, these parents are trying to do everything they can to let their two-year-old daughter know that they love her just as much as ever. While posing for a group picture, they even turn the baby away from her, so she can ignore it. Her father is smiling at her and tickling her tummy; her mother is also smiling and leaning toward her. All to little avail. Betsy's expression tells us that she is not fooled and knows that something important and disturbing has happened.

Feeling Small in a Large World

It is important to realize how small children feel among adults who are giants compared to them. Their surroundings can also appear immense.

It is all too easy to dominate a child by sheer size. Whole books have been written on the effects politicians, businessmen, and other aggressive people can achieve by making sure that they can "talk down" to others, be it from an elevated platform, a high chair like a throne, or simply by standing while others must sit.

The animal world offers many examples of their instinctive knowledge about dominating by height.

Cats will arch their backs to appear taller and will try to occupy the highest vantage point when they find themselves in unknown surroundings.

One-year-old Chris is looking up wistfully at his father, who seems to be unaware of how tall he appears to his son. Chris is preparing to get his father's attention by the movement of his left hand; possibly by pinching him. That should bring his father down to his level and available for what Chris wants to tell him!

National and cultural differences in body language can cause some misunderstandings. There is an aspect of this issue which may lead to unexpected difficulties: how much so-called body space does each person need? How close can you come to a child before he or she will feel uneasy?

Without realizing it, we all learn the socially acceptable distances for an encounter with strangers, another for members of a family; and yet another for intimate relationships. But there are big individual differences too: some children will feel threatened by "normal" approaches and are apt to react with panic,

withdrawal, or even violence. Some tests have shown that the more body space a person needs, the more he is likely to use violence to protect it.

Three-year-old Jack is being scolded by his mother. But she is doing more; she is also crowding him. This makes him uncomfortable. He would rather flee than listen to her. She would be more effective facing him from a distance of two or three feet. Closeness should be reserved for positive feelings. When closeness is combined with negative words, it creates an atmosphere of confusion and contradiction.

Practicing What You Preach

Attitudes about work are also transmitted continuously and effectively. Even though parents preach about the sanctity of work, a mother who cooks and cleans with a martyred expression or a father who just collapses in front of the TV set on weekends should not be astonished if their children don't like to do their own chores or study.

Two-year-old Debbie likes to help her mother hang up the laundry in the nice fresh air, because her mother does it with pleasure.

If a parent doesn't really enjoy physical activity, there is little chance that a small child will like it either.

Four-year-old Russell's father never made speeches to him about the virtues of exercise. But the father is an athletic, outgoing person and has roughhoused with his son practically since he was born. No wonder Russell has become a sturdy, unafraid child, and no wonder he can hardly wait for his father to come home.

Parents who learn to use body language effectively for both understanding and teaching their children will be rewarded by better communication with their children.

AUTHOR'S NOTE

After I had the idea for this book, I started to look through my files containing the thousands of photographs I have taken over the past twenty-five years. The pictures themselves suggested new avenues of thought; the repeated appearance of certain gestures reinforced the universality and importance of the children's body language.

A tear can have many causes; but I was there, and I knew why that child had cried. I felt that by adding my words to the photographs, I could produce a unique guide to the interpretation of children's behavior.

In some cases, I had followed the development of an individual child for years; in other instances, I photographed them only once. I especially enjoyed the longer relationships that sprang up between me and my subjects as I candidly documented their lives.

When I work, I use as much time and as little equipment as possible. This allows things to happen in a normal way. I let the children react to their parents and environment and everyday problems with no interference on my part.

I have learned a great deal by avidly reading the work of psychologists and psychoanalysts I respected, and by keeping attuned to what was *really* going on in the lives of my subjects. I owe a tremendous debt to those who allowed me to understand and love "my" substitute children.